Crazy Weather

W9-AOC-517

Written by David Drew
Illustrated by Susan Swan

Celebration Press
An Imprint of Pearson Learning

Today is

Sunday	Monday	Tuesday	Wednesday	Thursday	Friday	Saturday

Today's weather: **rainy**

Today's temperature:

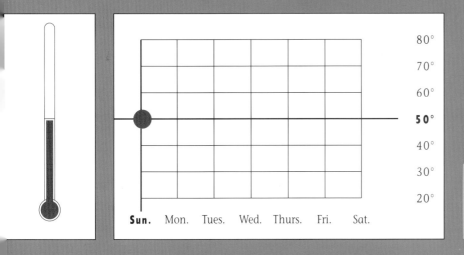

						80°
						70°
						60°
●						**50°**
						40°
						30°
						20°

Sun. Mon. Tues. Wed. Thurs. Fri. Sat.

50 °

Today's rainfall:

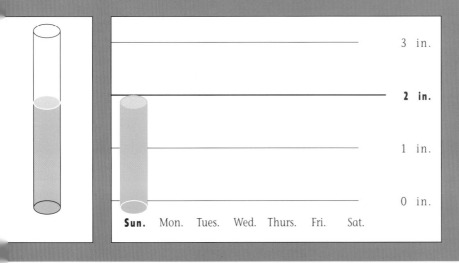

3 in.

2 in.

1 in.

0 in.

Sun. Mon. Tues. Wed. Thurs. Fri. Sat.

2 in.

Tomorrow's forecast

Today is

Sunday	Monday	Tuesday	Wednesday	Thursday	Friday	Saturday

Today's weather: **cloudy**

Today's temperature:

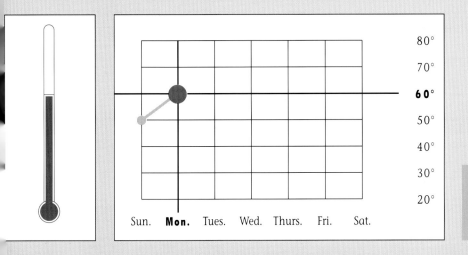

60 °

Today's rainfall:

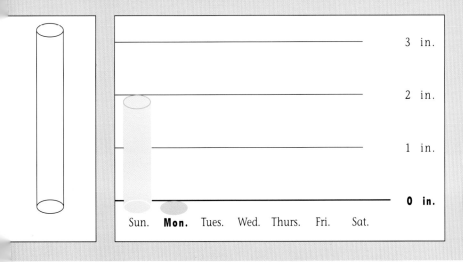

0 in.

Tomorrow's forecast

5

Today is

Sunday	Monday	Tuesday	Wednesday	Thursday	Friday	Saturday

Today's weather: **windy**

Today's temperature:

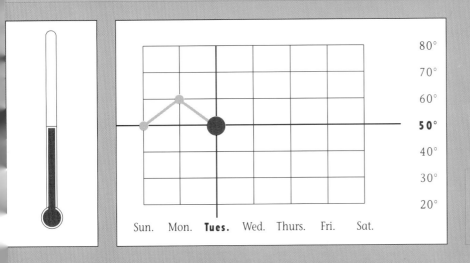

80°
70°
60°
50°
40°
30°
20°

Sun. Mon. **Tues.** Wed. Thurs. Fri. Sat.

50 °

Today's rainfall:

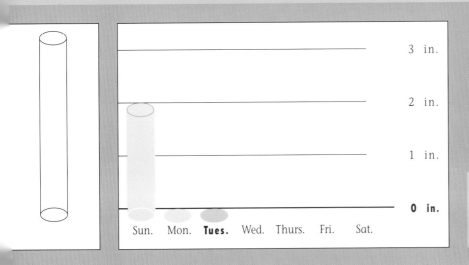

3 in.
2 in.
1 in.
0 in.

Sun. Mon. **Tues.** Wed. Thurs. Fri. Sat.

0 in.

Tomorrow's forecast

Today is

Sunday	Monday	Tuesday	Wednesday	Thursday	Friday	Saturday

Today's weather: **foggy**

8

Today's temperature:

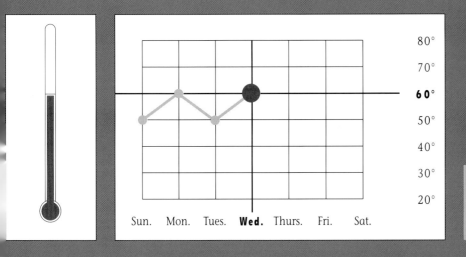

60 °

Today's rainfall:

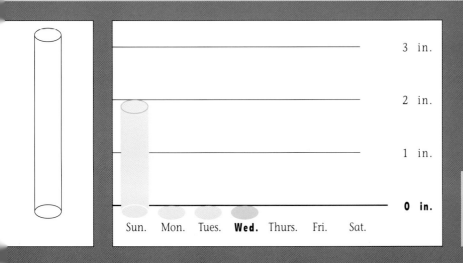

0 in.

Tomorrow's forecast

9

Today is

Sunday	Monday	Tuesday	Wednesday	Thursday	Friday	Saturday

Today's weather: **snowy**

Today's temperature:

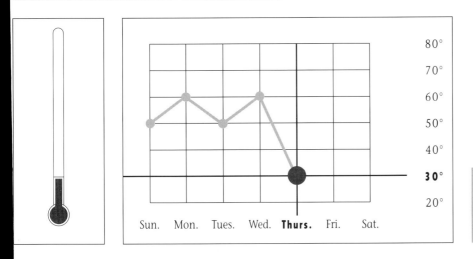

30 °

Today's snowfall:

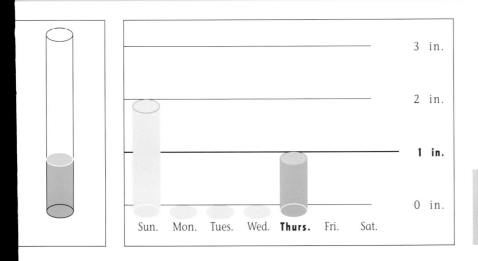

1 in.

Tomorrow's forecast

11

Today is

Sunday	Monday	Tuesday	Wednesday	Thursday	Friday	Saturday

Today's weather: **stormy**

Today's temperature:

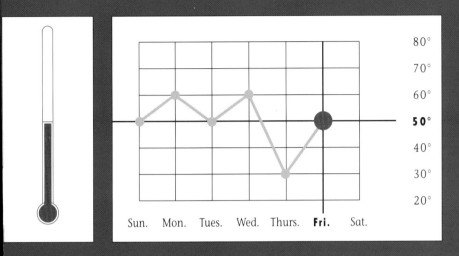

Sun.	Mon.	Tues.	Wed.	Thurs.	**Fri.**	Sat.

80°
70°
60°
50°
40°
30°
20°

50 °

Today's rainfall:

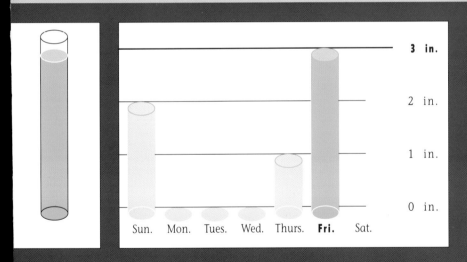

Sun.	Mon.	Tues.	Wed.	Thurs.	**Fri.**	Sat.

3 in.
2 in.
1 in.
0 in.

3 in.

Tomorrow's forecast

Today is

Sunday	Monday	Tuesday	Wednesday	Thursday	Friday	Saturday

Today's weather: **sunny**

Today's temperature:

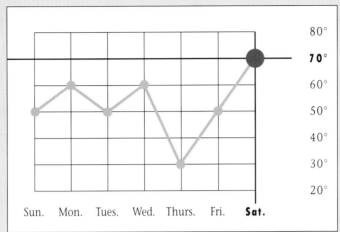

Sun.	Mon.	Tues.	Wed.	Thurs.	Fri.	**Sat.**

80°
70°
60°
50°
40°
30°
20°

70 °

Today's rainfall:

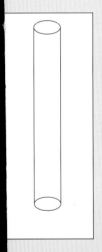
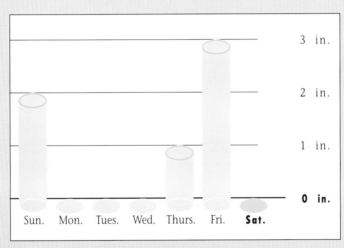

3 in.
2 in.
1 in.
0 in.

Sun.	Mon.	Tues.	Wed.	Thurs.	Fri.	**Sat.**

0 in.

This week's weather

Sunday	Monday	Tuesday	Wednesday	Thursday	Friday	Saturday

Temperatures

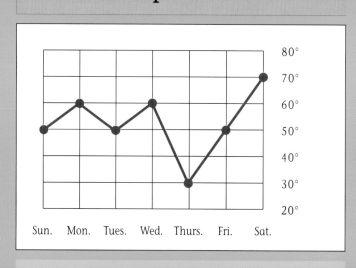

Rainfall

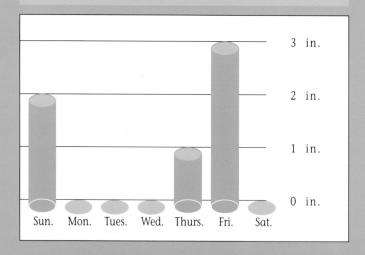

16